R. J. Elliott

History of Miss Annie Jones
Barnum's Esau Lady

ISBN/EAN: 9783337866068

Printed in Europe, USA, Canada, Australia, Japan

Cover: Foto ©ninafisch / pixelio.de

More available books at **www.hansebooks.com**

R. J. Elliott

History of Miss Annie Jones

Barnum's Esau Lady

HISTORY

OF

Miss Annie Jones,

BARNUM'S

Esau Lady.

Examine the Contents.

INTRODUCTION.

In reading the career of this remarkable lady I have no doubt that many will express the opinion that it is not true. My friends, I can safely say that every word as written in this little book is written on facts, scenes and incidents that actually occurred and can be verified; searched the criminal records of Connecticut, for the year 1867, and you will find the full account of the arrest and conviction of one Prof. Franklin for abduction, and you will find that he was sentenced to ten years' hard labor in the penitentiary, for the offense of stealing the daughter of Margaret Jones, a child about two years of age, and for the truth of this little history I refer you to any prominent show-manager in America. Believing that truth is what you seek, and that it will be just as interesting as fiction, I have confined myself to facts, and have not tried to enlarge on the adventures of this lady. In traveling exhibitions time is not afforded the lecturer to give a full and accurate description of each curiosity, consequently this little book is written to give you all the information you seek, and it is the only complete history of this lady ever written, and dates from birth to March, 1885.

Sincerely yours,

R. J. ELLIOTT.

HISTORY

OF

𝕸𝖎𝖘𝖘 𝕬𝖓𝖓𝖎𝖊 𝕵𝖔𝖓𝖊𝖘,

BARNUM'S ESAU LADY.

This remarkable lady is considered by scientific men and
students of Natural History to be one of the greatest wonders
in the known world. She first saw the light of day in the
beautiful little town of Marion, Smith County, in the State
of Virginia, (situated on the East Tennessee, Virginia and
Georgia Rail Road) on the 14th of July, 1865. The hair on
her head at birth was two feet in length a slight growth of
beard on her face as well ; her parents tried every available
means to remove this hirsute appendage from the child's
face ; but all their efforts proved of no avail. On the day
of her birth, the news spread with great rapidity—people
gathered from far and near to see the little wonder, and the
mother could have amassed a fortune, for the house and
surroundings was filled daily, with people that offered almost any price to enable them to get a look at God's great
handiwork, but the mother would not allow any one to see
her, because she had never heard of so remarkable a freak of
nature, and she thought no one ought to see the child. At
first, Annie's parents were almost beside themselves with
grief. and considered it an affliction, but when she came to

develop, and they realized how wonderful she was made—perfect in form and intellect ; bright, active and intelligent ; their admiration and love was unbounded. Her pleasant, sweet disposition won every one to love her and bless the sweet little darling. Annie's mother had seven children, (nothing remarkable in connection with any of the others ;) her father had no beard, and the mother was the same as any ordinary lady.

When Annie attained the age of two years, her parents were offered large inducements to place her on exhibition. They would not consider the matter for one moment ; they having a fine farm, and Annie's father being a good mechanic, it was not necessary for to travel, as they were far happier in their little home than they could be in any other place ; however, one bright day in August, in the year 1867, there landed in the little town of Marion, a stranger, to all the inhabitants unknown, who enquired at the hotel for the house of Mr. Jones, being directed by the landlord he started at once, on his arrival there he asked to see Annie, and introduced himself as Mr. O. J. Ferguson, Manager of Barnum's American Museum, New York. The child being placed before him, he at once tried to arrange for her appearance in New York, offering a large sum of money for one years' engagement, and the expenses of her mother. The inducements were so great that she at last agreed on the condition that if she did not like it that she could return home at any time.

This was her DEBUT before the public, and would have proved far more successful for them but for the great fire that occured shortly after her arrival there. (Her first appearance was on November 29th,) it was on the 30th of March, 1868, a bitter cold night,) I presume many of my readers will remember it.) Terror stricken, the mother with her child rushed in her night clothes through the smoke and flames nearly suffocated, into the bitter cold air ; they barely escaped with their lives, losing all they possessed ; they then returned to their home in Virginia to rest, until Mr. Barnum could again place her on exhibition, in the meantime

Annie's father died, and to add to the grief of the mother Annie was stolen while playing in the yard with another little girl, who rushed into the house exclaiming, "Oh, run quick, a big man has taken dear little Annie in his arms and climbed over the fence, and run away with her." Strict search was made by the neighbors, but they could gain no trace of the villian nor child, and the only description they had of him, was that given by the little girl, and that was "a big man." Annie was concealed from her mother for seven months; words cannot express her grief at this second bereavement; every exertion to find her proved of no avail. Annie's mother and P. T. Barnum telegraphed to all parts of the world to find her, but met with no success; Annie's mother had spent a small fortune, and only for the intervention of a good kind lady, would probably never had been able to recover her little darling.

With unwearied and untiring exertion she travelled from place to place, with her little boy, (nine years of age,) who mourned the loss of his little sister, constantly asking, "mama, when will I see my little sister Annie?" "soon, I hope," was the wearied mother's reply. Almost exhausted with fatigue, she stopped to obtain food for her little boy; not caring to eat, herself, she asked the lady if she could rest herself; the good woman acceded kindly and invited her to remain as long as she choose. Her natural intuition led her to believe that some great sorrow shadowed the pale and wearied mother; she asked her the cause of her great grief, in a few words she told of her loss; this good kind christain woman at once spoke cheering words to her, and told her she believed she knew the villian that stole her child, and that she should remain in her house until the proof of his villany and the truth of her words should be authenticated. Annie's mother waited and listened with breathless silence, which was only broken by her sobs, for she was almost beside herself with joy at the thought of once more clasping her little darling in her arms. The villian that stole Annie was a travelling phrenologist, calling himself Prof. Franklin, and the lady that gave Annie's mother the priceless informa.

tion was cousin to him, and employed by him as an Amanu-ensis. She was momently expecting a letter from him that would inform her of his whereabouts, as he wished her to write out his handbills as he had a little bearded girl that would prove a great acquisition to his lectures. This das-tardly act was proven only too true to her, and her surprise was so great and so mortifying she denounced him to Annie's mother at once, and told her to remain and she would give her the letter that would be proof ; that it would enable her to obtain possession of her child at once.

Annie's mother waited with breathless anxiety ; sleep and rest was out of the question. The much looked for letter came, and on its receipt was handed to the mother ; it stated that he was in Connecticut. Annie's mother lost no time in hastening to that place ; she immediately procured the ser-vices of an officer and found him at a hotel with Annie in his possession, he introduced her as his child. The officer having in his possession a warrant, without question imme-diately arrested and took him to the Court house, he still in-sisting it was his child. The judge took Annie's mother into his private office and told her "if the child knew her she could obtain possession of it without any further trouble, otherwise she must regain the child through the process of a law suit." The mother answered, "She is so young and has been gone so long she may have forgotten me." The judge then requested her to give a full description of her, which was given, and coincided with her appearance except the hair, which Annie's mother said hung in flowing curls to her feet, but the villian had cut it off her head and burnt the l ttle darling in two places, one on her cheek and the calf of her limb, so as to avoid detection if possible. When the mother entered the court-room where Annie was stand-ing, Annie immediately sprang forward, throwing her little arms up, faintly screamed "Oh there is my mamma, going to take me home away from this bad man, who burnt me mamma, and cut my hair off?" The judge told her "to take her child and wished her much joy and happiness, and that she might never have occasion to pass through such a terrible ordeal again."

The mother was overjoyed to once more clasp her little pet in her arms, and the good people of the place showed their enthusiasm for her in various ways. They contributed $300 for little Annie, also gave a splendid supper to her mother in honor of her regaining her lost child, which was the first the mother had enjoyed, during the whole seven months that Annie had been gone. They immediately started for their home, and on their way a venerable looking gentl- men, who having traveled some hours on the train with them, approached the mother and asked her "why the child was so closely veiled." Annie's mother told him who she was ; he told her "he was a showman and would like to see her, that he had heard of her strange adventures. The mother fearing a repetition of her past troubles utterly refused. The gentleman offered her one hundred dollars ; the mother consented, he gave the money without any hesitation, and pronounced her the greatest wonder he had ever heard of, and said "she was a veritable little Esau." From that time until the present she has been before the public, known as "the Infant Esau," "Esau Girl" and "Esau Lady." The gentleman's name was Major Burrell. His museum was situated on 5th avenue, Pittsburgh, Pa.; he placed her on exhibition. There is where she remained for eighteen months, exciting the wonder and admiration of the vast amount of visitors ; going to school in the morning and on exhibition afternoon and night ; her studies were a great pleasure to her. On one occasion her mother thought the task was too much for the child, and spoke of taking her away from school ; she cried so hard, that her mother with reluctance gave her consent to continue. In this manner, and by private schooling, she has received an accomplished education ; that combined with her many years of travel, renders her a brilliant conversationalist, which has made her many steadfast friends in all parts of the United States ; in fact there is no city of any prominence but what she has her many friends and admirers ; she is a favorite with all who come in contact with her ; growing more beautiful every day, her beard is as soft as silk and beautiful in color, "a rich chesnut brown;" her skin is clear pink and white and like velvet; her hair does not curl as it did when she was a child, before it was cut off, but reaches within a few inches of the ground. Some might say, that far back her relations perhaps, were of the same bearded nature; her ancestors can be traced back for centuries, none of which inherited this remarkable peculiarity; she is the only one, and history gives no account of such an extraordinary freak of nature. Her voice is sweet and effeminate; an accomplished vocalist. She quick and impulsive in nature, and most industrious in her ways; many ladies have beautiful pieces of her handiwork, which she accomplished in her leisure hours; a perfect guide of colors and an excellent memory, with vivid imagination.

After remaining on exhibition in Pittsburgh the eighteen months, she was engaged by a traveling showman. named Dr. E. Backenstoe for a like period, which also proved very successful, and after traveling over a large part of the United States, and receiving excellent notices from the press, she at the expiration of her engagement returns once more to her old friend and manager, Mr. P. T. Barnum; that was the year 1871, and the first season of the great Barnum show, or as it was called, "The World's Fair." traveling by wagons through the New England States, receiving a large salary, also the profits on her photographs and books, selling a vast amount of each, being on exhibition in the large show and advertised very extensively as one of the leading attract ons, viz; "Barnum's Infant Esau." At the close of the season of 1871, which occured in October, she returned to Virginia to remain until spring, being engaged by Mr. Barnum for the season of 1872, (and I would here remark that in 1871 Mr. Barnum was the one to inaugurate the plan of a museum in connection with a circus and menagerie,)

In the spring, he placed on the road the first large Rail Road Show; they started early in April, showing in all the prominent cities of the East and West, and proved a most successful season. Traveling by rail road, they found it far more comfortable, having a good night's rest instead of traveling all night in a carriage. In the month of July, Mr. Barnum re-engaged Annie for the following year; at the close of the season of 1882 Annie and her mother was engaged for the winter season to travel South with the Barnum Company, opening in Louisville late in October, (the summer season closing in Detroit, Mich.,) owing to extreme bad weather, cold, rain and snow, which caused many valuable animals to die. The Company closed after a few weeks, in New Orleans, La., going into winter quarters in Algiers, opposite N. O.

Annie and her mother went from there to Boston, Mass., remaining their all winter, resting; in April, 1873, opening in Brooklyn, N. Y., for four days with "Barnum's Greatest Show on Earth," this season showing in nearly all the same cities and towns as the previous. The business was phenomenal, and Barnum's name became a household word; up to that time it had the largest biz ever known, but it has increased from year to year until there appeared to be no limit; to return to our subject, at the close of the season of 1873, Annie's mother, in conjunction with a showman run a traveling museum through the Eastern States, which proved fairly successful.

In the Spring of 1874 she was engaged by G. B. Bunnell to travel with the Buckley Hippodrome, starting from Delevan, Wis., May 7th, and traveling five months, closing the season (of the side-show) at Cleveland, O. Mr. Bunnell also having the privilege with the Barnum Hippodrome, took his side-show and joined them in Pittsburgh, remaining two weeks, then to Cincinnati, for a like period. In the Spring of 1875 joined Uffner and Norman, they having the side-show with the America's Racing Association and Hippodrome, starting from Cincinnati, April 1st. After three month's of a disastrious season closed in Ogdensburg. N. Y., resting all that winter. In the spring, Annie and her mother traveled through the Eastern States once more, and were very successful; in the fall returning to New York and resting all winter.

In the spring of 1877 she was employed by Mr. J. L. Hutchinson for Howe's Great London Show, which proved a successful season for Annie and her mother, and on returning to New York were engaged for the winter season at Jacobs and Tillottson's New York Museum, remaining there until the spring of 1878 ; then once more on the road with Mr. Hutchinson and the London Show. This season was fairly successful, returning to New York in the fall, and was once more engaged by Jacobs, Tillottson and Bunnell for one year, they having consolidated their museums in New York ; remained in that city from October 1878 until the fall of 1879, then H. R. Jacobs and G. B. Bunnell started a traveling museum through the East, which proved a great success ; remaining from one to two weeks in each city, visiting New Haven, Conn., Providence, R. I., Hartford, Conn., Worcester, Mass., Albany, N. Y., Troy, N. Y., and many other cities, returning to New York, and opening in Brooklyn for a long season. In the spring of 1880 joined the Pullman and Hamilton Show at St. Catharines, Canada, Mr. Jacobs having the privileges ; remained with them until September, then Mr. Jacobs left the Company with his Side Show for the Fairs, leaving the P. and H. Show at Winterport, Maine ; going by boat to Boston, thence by rail to the New England Fair at Worcester, thence to Waverly, Freehold, Flemington, Mount Holly, in New Jersey, and Doylestown, Pa., and doing a tremendous biz ; remained in New York all that winter on exhibition - was engaged by Mr. J. L. Hutchinson for the Barnum and London United Shows, appearing in April, 1881, which was the largest season's receipts Annie and her mother had ever had.

On the close of the season they returned to New York and was engaged by Mr. C. A. Bradenburg, Thomas Meal an and James Wilson, for their museum (the Globe,) for the season, and remained there until the opening of the Barnum London Shows at Madison Square Garden, March 13th. 1882. After a six week's season in New York, visited all the Eastern towns and cities, going as far West as Cleveland, Ohio. On returning to New York in the fall was engaged by

Bradenburg. Meahan and Wilson, and remained there all
season with the exception of four weeks at Herzog & Co's.
museum in Baltimore; opening there December 25th.

On the inauguration of the Barnum London Show at Madison Square Garden, in March, 1883. Annie went on exhibition with that Company for another season; after a successful season in New York visited all the Western cities; the privileges being under the management of Kohl, Hagar and Middleton, closing the most successful season Annie ever had, at Hannibal, Mo., October 20th, going from there to Cincinnati, Ohio, after a rest of several weeks, opened at P. Harris' museum, for three weeks, and from there to his Pittsburgh museum for a season of four weeks, closing in Pittsburgh, December 22d, and opening at Hagar, Campbell and Bradenburg's museum in Philadelphia, for three weeks, then to Drew's museum, Providence, R. L, then to Herzog & Co's Baltimore museum; after a rest of two weeks opened at Madison Square Garden, New York, with Barnum London Shows for the season of 1885, on March 10th.

In closing this brief history, I would say that Miss Annie is happy and contented, enjoys the best of health, and as you have seen, is perfect in form and features. As her destiny is in the hands of God, and may he temper her mind to follow the course in future the same as the past, is the sincere wish of all that know her, and in closing this sketch, kind reader, if you feel that you have received the full value of the small price you have invested, then we will consider we are amply repaid for the time and patience we have brought to bear in preparing it for you, and in behalf of Miss Annie I will bid you an affectionate farewell, not good-bye, for she is in hopes of meeting you often in the future.

The End.

By MISS ANNIE JONES.

"BEAU LADY."

I come, I come, ye have called me long,
I come from Virginia with light and song ;
Ye may tra ? me ever, o'er the wakening earth,
And the winds will whisper my gentle birth.

I have passed through the South in its genial hours,
And thousands of songsters, in the forest bowers have
      heralded my coming ;
They are bursting fresh from their sparry cares,
And the earth resound with the joy of wares.

I have roamed o'er the hills of the stormy North,
Midst blinding sleet and snow ;
Whilst thousands have come from the forest and plain,
To see the bearded girl again.

Come forth, O, ye children of gladness, come
Where the violets lay, may be your home ;
Ye, of the posey and dew-bright eye,
And the bounding footsteps to greet me, fly !
Come with your parents, and sweethearts come,
My stay is short ; that I may bid you good-bye.

How to Draw and Paint.—A complete handbook on the

whole art of Drawing and Painting, containing concise instructions in Outline, Light and Shade, Perspective, Sketching from Nature, Figure Drawing, Artistic Anatomy, Landscape, Marine, and Portrait Painting, the principles of colors applied to paintings, etc., etc., with over 100 illustrations. 12mo, boards, with cloth back ... .50 cts.

Excelsior Series of Recitations and Readings.—The

great demand for new and suitable Readings and Recitations has le l to the compilation of these books. Our experience of the past war rants the belief that our efforts will be appreciated by the public Each number will contain about 176 pages, bound in a beautiful illustrated cover printed in colors. Nos. 1, 2, 3, and 4 now ready; contents sent free on application.. .. ..25 cts. each.

The Complete Debater. Containing Debates, Outlines

of Debates, and Questions for Discussion, to which is added an original and complete debate on Free Trade. Bound in boards, with cloth back, containing over 200 pages.......... .... 50 cts.

The Modern Bartender's Guide.—Containing clear

and practical directions for mixing all kinds of cocktails, sours, egg nogs, sherry cobblers, coolers, absinthe, crustas, fizzes, flips, juleps, fixes, punches, lemonades, and ponsse cafés, together with complete directions and receipts for making all kinds of domestic brandies, beer wines, cordials, extracts, and syrups. Bound in paper........ ..50 cts. Bound in extra cloth, gilt ... .75 cts.

Payne's Business Letter Writer and Book of Commercial Forms.—Containing specimen letters on all possible

business topics, with appropriate answers. Added to this are a great number of forms for Business Papers and Documents, such as Agreements, Leases, Promissory Notes, Mortgages, Bonds, Receipts, and a host of other forms. Bound in boards, with cloth back..........50 cts.

Dunbar's Complete Hand-book of Etiquette.—This

work presents, in a clear and intelligible manner, the whole art and philosophy of Etiquette. Among the contents are: Bodily Deportment, Speak Grammatically, Self Respect, Pedantry, Social Characters, Traveling, Useful Hints on Conversation, etc., etc. Bound in boards, cloth back........................ ....50 cts.

Burdett's Irish Dialect Recitations and Readings.—

This new collection of rare Irish sketches, in prose and verse, arranged for public representation, embraces the most sparkling Irish wit, set forth with the irresistible humor of Irish brogue. Illuminated paper cover ... .25 cts.

www.ingramcontent.com/pod-product-compliance
Lightning Source LLC
Chambersburg PA
CBHW031159090426
42738CB00008B/1395